# INDIAN TALK

## *HAND SIGNALS OF THE AMERICAN INDIANS*

By

**Iron Eyes Cody**

© Copyright, 1970
by Naturegraph Company

Illustrated by Ken Mansker, Flathead Indian Artist

Posed by Iron Eyes, Yeawas, Robert and Arthur

Paper Edition   ISBN 0-911010-82-3
Cloth Edition   ISBN 0-911010-83-1

Naturegraph Publishers, Happy Camp, California 96039

Iron Eyes with his wife Yeawas and their sons Robert and Arthur. Family pet Mitzie Sapa. Iron Eyes' tipis in the background.

## * * * TABLE OF CONTENTS * * *

**FULL**        **DOG**        **DRINK**

I dedicate this book to my two sons, Robert and Arthur and to the youth of America in the hope that it will serve as an incentive ot keep alive this early form of Indian talk.

Iron Eyes Cody

## AMERICAN INDIAN "SIGN-TALK"

What is "sign-talk"?  All of us use a little of it.  For us, nodding the head means "yes", shaking it "no"; a finger pressed against the lips means "don't say anything". But it took the Indians of the American Plains area to concoct a real "sign language" by which a whole conversation can be carried on without saying a word. The object was to make it possible for tribes speaking different languages to communicate with each other.

Iron Eyes, the author of this book, is a Cherokee, an eastern tribe who did not use "sign talk"; but Plains Indian friends of his father taught him, and eventually after traveling among many tribes, he became expert.

With my own eyes I have seen a Kiowa and a Cheyenne, on the streets of Anadarko, Oklahoma, carry on a long conversation without making a sound!

I have known Iron Eyes and Yeawas for many years, and they are good friends of mine. The basement of their home is a real museum of Indian costumes, weapons, and ornaments.  Because of his knowledge and ability, ]Iron Eyes spends much of his time as a technical advisor on Indian matters for various movie and television concerns, and acts Indian parts in the shows themselves.

M. R. Harrington
Curator Emeritus
Southwest Museum

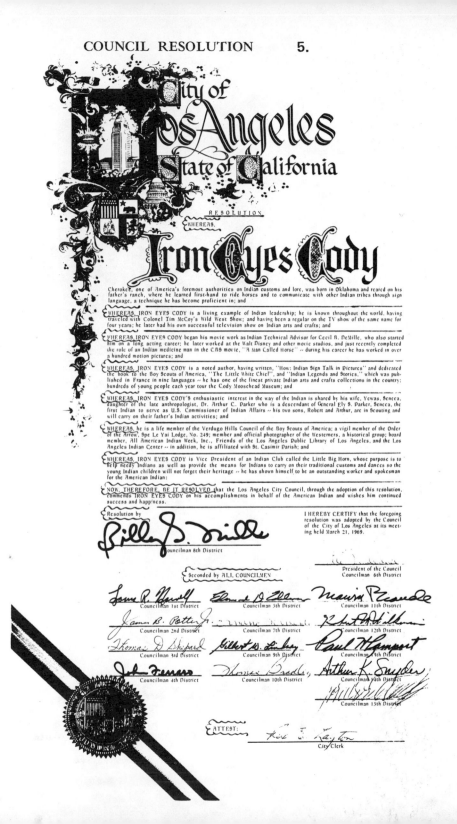

# City of Los Angeles
## State of California

RESOLUTION

WHEREAS,

# Iron Eyes Cody

Cherokee, one of America's foremost authorities on Indian customs and lore, was born in Oklahoma and reared on his father's ranch, where he learned first-hand to ride horses and to communicate with other Indian tribes through sign language, a technique he has become proficient in; and

WHEREAS, IRON EYES CODY is a living example of Indian leadership; he is known throughout the world, having traveled with Colonel Tim McCoy's Wild West Show; and having been a regular on the TV show of the same name for four years; he later had his own successful television show on Indian arts and crafts; and

WHEREAS, IRON EYES CODY began his movie work as Indian Technical Advisor for Cecil B. DeMille, who also started him on a long acting career; he later worked at the Walt Disney and other movie studios, and just recently completed the role of an Indian medicine man in the CBS movie, "A Man Called Horse" -- during his career he has worked in over a hundred motion pictures; and

WHEREAS, IRON EYES CODY is a noted author, having written, "How: Indian Sign Talk in Pictures" and dedicated the book to the Boy Scouts of America, "The Little White Chief", and "Indian Legends and Stories," which was published in France in nine languages -- he has one of the finest private Indian arts and crafts collections in the country; hundreds of young people each year tour the Cody Mooschead Museum; and

WHEREAS, IRON EYES CODY'S enthusiastic interest in the way of the Indian is shared by his wife, Yewas, Seneca, daughter of the late anthropologist, Dr. Arthur C. Parker who is a descendant of General Ely S. Parker, Seneca, the first Indian to serve as U.S. Commissioner of Indian Affairs -- his two sons, Robert and Arthur, are in Scouting and will carry on their father's Indian activities; and

WHEREAS, he is a life member of the Verdugo Hills Council of the Boy Scouts of America; a vigil member of the Order of the Arrow, Spe Le Yai Lodge, No. 249; member and official photographer of the Westerners, a historical group; board member, All American Indian Week, Inc., Friends of the Los Angeles Public Library of Los Angeles, and the Los Angeles Indian Center -- in addition, he is affiliated with St. Casimir Parish; and

WHEREAS, IRON EYES CODY is Vice President of an Indian Club called the Little Big Horn, whose purpose is to help needy Indians as well as provide the means for Indians to carry on their traditional customs and dances so the young Indian children will not forget their heritage -- he has shown himself to be an outstanding worker and spokesman for the American Indian;

NOW, THEREFORE, BE IT RESOLVED that the Los Angeles City Council, through the adoption of this resolution, commends IRON EYES CODY on his accomplishments in behalf of the American Indian and wishes him continued success and happiness.

Resolution by

*Billy G. Mills*
Councilman 8th District

I HEREBY CERTIFY that the foregoing resolution was adopted by the Council of the City of Los Angeles at its meeting held March 21, 1969.

President of the Council
Councilman 6th District

Seconded by ALL COUNCILMEN

*Louis R. Nowell*
Councilman 1st District

*James B. Potter Jr.*
Councilman 2nd District

*Thomas D. Shepard*
Councilman 3rd District

*John Ferraro*
Councilman 4th District

*Edmund D. Edelman*
Councilman 5th District

Councilman 7th District

*Gilbert W. Lindsay*
Councilman 9th District

*Thomas Bradley*
Councilman 10th District

*Marvin Braude*
Councilman 11th District

*Robert J. Wilkinson*
Councilman 12th District

*Paul H. Lamport*
Councilman 14th District

*Arthur K. Snyder*
Councilman 14th District

Councilman 15th District

ATTEST:

City Clerk

Iron Eyes and Col. Tim McCoy doing signs "Night is long.

Iron Eyes, Sitting Bull's son, Yeawas, doing signs "My heart,            friend,            is good."

## IRON EYES CODY

Iron Eyes Cody's father was a Cherokee Indian named Thomas Long Plume, who toured with a wild west show. At an early age, Iron Eyes joined his father and, while traveling throughout the United States and Canada, had the opportunity to visit many different Indian tribes.

His father's friends, Two Gun White Calf, a Blackfoot Indian, and Buffalo Man, a Cheyenne Indian, taught Iron Eyes basic sign language, this helped him to communicate with the various tribes he visited. Later the great Arapaho Chief White Horse, taught Iron Eyes to improve his technic. His association and travel with his pal Colonel Tim McCoy, an expert in sign language, helped Iron Eyes to become the skillful communicator he is today.

Iron Eyes was an expert Indian dancer and he won many prizes and trophies during his travels with various shows. He felt highly honored when he was commanded to dance before the King and Queen of England.

He toured Australia with the Sydney Royal Agricultural Show. Archery being another one of his specialities, he hunted wild boar and kangaroo with his bow and arrows, and had many interesting adventures with the Bushmen of that country. He also won the 40-yard trophy from the Melbourne Centenary Archery Association and the 40-yard trophy from the Coogee Archery Association, while in Australia.

Iron Eyes' home is always open to anyone interested in Indian lore. His "Moosehead Museum" is considered one of the best private Indian collections in the United States. Numerous youth groups have visited his basement museum, and have learned how to make copies of authentic costumes, Indian dancing, singing as well as sign language.

Iron Eyes' vocation is portraying the American Indian in motion pictures and television. He is also a technical advisor on Indian customs, language, songs and dances, and has furnished authentic costumes and props from his private collection for many an Indian picture.

One of Iron Eyes' hobbies is photography, and he is rarely seen without his camera. The pictures in this book have been taken by him, developed and printed in his basement dark room.

He has photographed many Indian ceremonials, where allowed, throughout the United States. He has attended the Sun Dance in South Dakota and for many years the Hopi Snake Dance and other ceremonies in Arizona and New Mexico. He has served as Master of Ceremony for the Grand Council of American Indians in Gary, Indiana, and the Confederated Tribes of American Indians in Milwaukee, Wisconsin and for many other Indian pow-wows.

Iron Eyes has written many newspaper and magazine articles on the American Indian. His first book "How Indian Sign Talk in Pictures," now out of print, was used by the Boy Scouts of America. A second book titled "Indian Rituals" will be published in France and translated into nine foreign languages. He is currently preparing with Yeawas a book on American Indian legends, stories which she related on the Iron Eyes Tipi television show.

The City of Los Angeles honored Iron Eyes by presenting him with a colorful resolution plaque, stating all his qualifications and ending with the words: "NOW, THEREFORE, BE IT RESOLVED that the Los Angeles City Council, through the adoption of this resolution commends IRON EYES CODY on his accomplishments in behalf of the American Indian and wishes him continued success and happiness." Adopted March 21, 1969 and signed by all Councilmen.

Iron Eyes is an active member on the Board of the Los Angeles Indian Center; The Friends of the Los Angeles Library Association; vice-president of the Little Big Horn American Indian Club; board member and photographer for The Los Angeles Corral of The Westerners, a historical club; and a Life Member of the Verdugo Council of the Boy Scouts of America; and Vigil Member of the Spe-Le-Yai Lodge 249 of the Order of the Arrow in Glendale, California.

He is married to Yeawas, daughter of the late Dr. Arthur C. Parker, Seneca Indian and famous anthropologist and founder of National Indian Day. Her great, great, great uncle was General Ely S. Parker, the first Indian to become Commissioner of Indian Affairs. She was born on an archeological expedition in New York.

His two sons, Robert, 18, and Arthur, 16, are champion Indian dancers, and well trained in traditional Indian customs. They understand and speak Cherokee, sign language and can sing many different tribal songs, as well as perform various tribal dances. They are sports minded and Life Scouts. Robert is a Blood Brother of the Spe-Le Yai Lodge 239 of the Order of the Arrow.

Sign language is slowly passing on with the old timers and Iron Eyes hopes that the youth of today will find it interesting enough to keep it alive for future generations to enjoy.

Iron Eyes with former Commissioner of Indian Affairs Robert L. Bennett, an Oneida Indian, who was the second American Indian to ever hold this office.

### Notes on the Sign Language

Sign language is used throughout the world in many forms, by those who cannot hear, in sports, in training animals, in games and in many other ways. However communication by "hand-sign" was used by the American Indians before the coming of the "white man." One reason being, that there were hundreds of distinct languages being spoken by some fifty-six distinct linguistic families.

Just who invented sign language is not known. Its greatest development was among the Plains buffalo-hunting Indians, with the Kiowa Indians being the most proficient in the art.

There are many minor differences among the various tribes. Most signs were originated due to the necessity to communicate with various wandering tribes while engaged in hunting.

This method of communication was also useful to warriors in battle, in which signs would be given over sighting distance, to surprise an enemy.

Chiefs in council found this method an attention attractor, in that the listeners would have to pay strict attention in order to get the message.

It would take thousands of illustrations and words to compile the entire vocabulary of the American Indian sign language, so only the most simple and common signs have been used in this book.

ABOARD

ACHE

1. **ABOARD:** Hold left palm up, place heel of right fist on left palm. Means also *sitting down on.*

2. **ABOVE:** Place right palm on back of left hand, fingers in opposite directions, raise right hand upward to indicate distance.

3. **ACHE:** Move vertical right index finger up and down chest. Means also *throbbing sensation of pain.*

ABOVE

ACROSS

AFRAID

4. **ACROSS:** Pass the right hand, in a curve-like motion, over the back of the left hand.

*ADD: Place right palm on left palm, fingers in opposite directions, pull up slightly, repeat two or three times. Means* **piling up.**

5. **AFRAID:** Elbows out, pull curved index fingers toward chest. Means *pulling in your horns,* or *cowardly.*

6. **AFTER:** Hold palm of left hand up, with right index finger on left palm draw an imaginary line down past the wrist. Or, with the right index finger, draw along the length of the pointed left index finger down past the wrist. Also means *behind* or *late.*

AFTER

ALIKE

ALL

7. **ALIKE:** Point right index and middle fingers downward to palm of left hand. Also means *resemble* or *twins*.
*ALIVE: See alone.*

8. **ALL:** Make a horizontal circle with right hand, palm down.

9. **ALL GONE:** Palms of hands facing body, fingers in opposite directions. Brush right hand across left palm and swing outward.

ALL GONE

ALONE

ANGRY

10. **ALONE:** Place upright index finger in center of neck, then move finger away in a jerking motion. To indicate *alive,* do above motion but only zigzag the finger.
     *ALSO: See equal.*

11. **ANGRY:** Place closed right fist in middle of forehead, with thumb touching head, and make a circular motion clockwise.

12. **ANTELOPE:** Place thumbs and extended index fingers at base of ears.

ANTELOPE

APACHE

ARISE

13. **APACHE:** Do sign for Indian, then with the right index finger rub the left index from the end of finger to the wrist and back again two or three times. Means *Elk-horn fiddlers.*

*APART: See separate.*

*APPLE: Do sign for tree, thumbs and forefingers indicate size of fruit, point to something red then do sign for eat.*

*ARGUE: See quarrel.*

14. **ARISE:** Point right index finger downward, palm up, then bring upward.

15. **ARRIVED HERE:** Hold up left hand, palm facing body, touch back of left hand with right index finger.

ARRIVE HERE

ARRIVE THERE

ASTONISHED

**16. ARRIVED THERE:** With right index finger, touch the palm of the left upright hand.

*ARROW: Cup left hand near breast, then make a motion with right hand as if drawing an arrow from left hand.*

**17. ASTONISHED:** Place right hand over mouth, pull upraised left hand in toward face.

**18. AT:** Extend left hand, palm down, place fingers of right hand on back of left.

*AWL: See sew.*

AT

AXE

BACON

19. **AXE:** Place left hand under elbow of right arm, bend right hand at wrist and making chopping-like motions.

*BABY: Cross arms, right arm next to body, close right hand.*

20. **BACON:** Hold out left hand and with right thumb and finger rub up and down heel of left hand, then do sign for eat.

21. **BAD:** Hold clenched right fist up on left breast, pull away and open hand and make casting away motion downward and toward right side. Also means *evil.*

BAD

BAG

BEAR

**22. BAG:** Extend left hand, vertical position, cup fingers, push folded right fingers down past curve of left hand.

*BEAN: Extend palm of right hand, back down, with thumb, touch first joint of index finger.*

BEAUTIFUL

**23. BEAR:** Cup hands over ears, fingers pointing upward, ( indicates thick ears) then make clawing motions with both hands.

*BEARD:    See goat.*

**24. BEAUTIFUL:** Hold right hand in front of face, as if looking into a mirror, then make the sign for good.

BEAVER

BELOW

25. **BEAVER:** Hold right hand under palm of left hand, then bring back up and slap left palm two or three times, indicates sound of beaver tail slapping on water or mud.
>*BEGIN: See push.*
>*BEHIND: See after.*

26. **BELOW:** Palms down, fingers in opposite directions, rest left hand on back of right hand drop right hand down a few inches.

BIG

27. **BIG:** Hold palms of hands toward each other, pull apart. Also means *great* or *wide*.
>*BIRD: Hold outspread fingers at each side of body, then make flapping motions.*

BIT

BLANKET

BOAT

**28. BIT:** Place thumb and forefinger of right hand across mouth. Also means *bridle.*

**29. BLANKET:** Place fists at shoulders, pull in toward center of body, as if pulling blanket around body.

*BLESS: Raise arms above head, palms forward, bring down toward person or food.*

**30. BOAT:** Cup hands together in boat-like shape, push forward. Do sign for rowing. *See canoe.*

BOOK

31.  **BOOK:**  Hold palms of hands together in vertical position, then open outward, little fingers touching.

32.  **BORN (or)  BIRTH :** With right hand make a sweeping motion under palm of left hand.

*BOWL: Cup both hands together in front of body in bowl-like shape.*

BORN

BOY

**33. BOY:** *(little)* Hold right index finger up, palm out, elbow by side, lower hand then bring upward. Means also *boy growing up.*

**34. BRAND:** Form a half circle with right thumb and index finger, place on left breast or on right hip. This sign is sometimes used to ask a person's name. Meaning *"What is your brand or name?"*

BRAND

BREAD

35. **BREAD:** Place right palm across left palm, reverse hand position, left on right, repeat. This is method of flattening flour cake for fry bread.

36. **BREAK:** Make a motion of breaking imaginary stick with both hands.

*BRIDLE: See bit.*

*BRING: Point index finger, back towards right, hook index finger in towards body.*

BREAK

BROTHER

BUFFALO

BUFFALO CALF

CALLED

37. **BROTHER:** Place right index and middle fingers at mouth (means *to nurse together*). Then do sign for man.

*BLOOD BROTHER: Place fingers under nostrils and bring down past mouth in a wavey-like motion. Then repeat sign for brother.*

*BROTHER-IN-LAW: Cross arms in front of chest, move right hand down past elbow of left arm.*


38. **BUFFALO:** Place thumbs in center of palms, close fingers around thumbs, then hold slightly curved hands above ears. Means *thick horns.*


39. **BUFFALO CALF:** Close fists and extend thumbs upward and place on either side of ears. Means *short stubby horns.*

*BUFFALO COW: Cup hands over ears, (sign for thick horns) then make milking motion.*

*BULLET: See cartridge.*

*BURDEN: Hold clenched hands over forehead, like holding a burden strap.*


40. **CALLED OR NAMED:** Place closed right hand by mouth, open fingers and push forward, point left index finger.

CAMP

CANOE

CANNOT

41. **CAMP:** Cross upraised index fingers in front of body. Represents tops of tipi poles.

42. **CANNOT:** Hold up left hand, palm towards right. With right index finger strike center of left palm. Pull right index finger back towards right, turning hand so back is down. Also means *fail* or *unable*.

43. **CANOE:** Clench hands over imaginary oar and make rowing motions to right. Or shape right hand like bow of canoe and push forward. Both signs may be used at the same time.

CANYON

CARRY

44. **CANYON:** Place fists, facing each other, on either side of face. (means *mountains on both sides*) Drop left fist to horizontal position and, with open right hand in vertical position, sweep under left fist. Means *passing through*. Also means *gorge*.

45. **CARRY:** Clasp hands over ends of imaginary bundle hanging from right shoulder.

46. **CARTRIDGE:** Close last three fingers of hand and touch last joint of right index finger with thumb. (Means *length of shell*) Make motion of shooting gun. Also means *bullet*.

CARTRIDGE

CAT

CENTER

CHERRIES

CHEYENNE

47. **CAT:** Flatten end of nose with right thumb and index finger to indicate flat nose of a cat.

48. **CENTER:** Point right index finger to middle joint of left index finger; or make a circle with thumb and index fingers and with right index finger point down in center half of circle of left hand.

*CHAIR: Hold left hand upright, place closed fist at base of palm. Means* **backrest.**

*CHEROKEE: Forest people. Do sign for trees, spread fingers held erect, then with right hand rub left back of hand to indicate Indian.*

49. **CHERRIES:** Do sign for tree, make picking motion, then pound on left palm. Motion of pounding choke cherries.

50. **CHEYENNE:** With right index finger make chopping motion on left index finger. They were called finger choppers, because they cut off a finger as a sign of mourning.

CHICKEN

CHIEF

CLOUDS

COFFEE

51.  **CHICKEN:**  Wave outspread fingers up and down, sign for bird, then place outspread fingers on top of head to indicate comb of bird.

52.  **CHIEF:**  Hold up fingers of left hand, palm out, pass right index finger over left fingers.  This means *"one man over all men, or chief."*

*CHILD:  Make sign for boy or girl, then extend right hand, palm down to indicate height of child.*

*CHOOSE:  See you.*

*CHURCH:  Place index fingers to form a cross, then touch index fingers to form shape of spire.*

*CITY:  See house.*

*CLOSE:  See near.*

53.  **CLOUDS:**  Touch finger-tips of both hands over head, then make a slow moving motion upward.

*COAT:  Place palms of hands on chest and brush downward to waist.  Also means* **clothes.**

54.  **COFFEE:**  Hold left palm upward, clench right hand and make a grinding motion over left, as if turning an old-fashioned coffee mill.

COIN

COLD

55. **COIN:** With right thumb and index finger form a circle. Also means *money.*

56. **COLD:** Place closed hands close to chest, shoulder high, then make a shivering motion.
 *COLOR: Rub tips of right hand on back of left hand, look for something that has the color you wish to indicate and point to it.*

COME

57. **COME:** Curve right index finger upward, then hook toward body.

COOK

58. **COOK:** Hands palm to palm, rub right palm in circle over left, then make a motion as if to place something in left hand and do the sign for fire.

59. **CORN:** Twist left thumb and index fingers with right fingers as if shelling corn.

*COUNCIL: Hold clench- ed hands in front of body, shoulder high, little fingers touching, pull apart and turn in an imaginary circle so that thumbs of fists are now touch- ing. Make sign for talk.*

*COUNTING AND NUM- BERS: See back of book.*

*COVERED WAGON: See wagon wheels.*

*COWARD: See afraid.*

CORN

CRY

CRADLEBOARD: *Hold arms to left side of body, palms facing body, right arm slightly lower.*

CRAZY: *See angry.*

CROW INDIAN: *Make sign for Indian and place closed hand, palm out at top of forehead. The latter indicates the pompadour style of hairdress.*

60. **CRY:** Point index fingers to inner corners of eyes and pull down. Means *tears falling.*

61. **CUT:** Make cutting motion with heel of right hand across palm of left hand.

CUT

DANCE

DAY

62. **DANCE:** Hold palms facing one another several inches apart, move hands up and down two or three times. Fingers represent people, movements of hands, dancing.

*DARE: See defy.*

63. **DAY:** Hold both hands in horizontal position, cross right over left to make a shadow (night), then turn palms upward, fingers pointing out. Means *night is finished and is opening.*

64. **DAYBREAK:** Hold palms of hands facing body, one above the other, with a small space between each one.

DAYBREAK

DEAF

DECISION

DEEP

**65. DEAF:** Press palm of hand over ear to close out sound, then do sign for no.

**66. DECISION:** Hold out left hand, palm up, with heel of right hand strike down and across left palm. Means *"I have decided."*

**67. DEEP:** Hold left hand down low, palm up; hold right hand, palm down, up high, then drop down towards left palm.

DEER

DEFY

**68. DEER:** Touch ears with thumbs, fingers outspread and pointing upward. Indicates antlers.

**69. DEFY:** Push thumb of right hand between right index and middle fingers. Also means *dare* or *challenge*.

*DESTROY: See exterminate.*

**70. DIE:** Hold out left hand, palm down, place right index finger to the left of extended hand, pull over to right and push down under palm. Means also *going under*.

DIE

DIG

DIRT

**71. DIG:** Curve hands downward and pull towards body in a digging motion.

**72. DIRT:** Point downward with right finger, reach down and rub imaginary dirt between fingers.

*DOCTOR: Do sign for medicine then sign for white man.*

**73. DOG:** Extend first two fingers of right hand and draw across body from left to right. Means *pulling a travois.* In the early days dogs were used to pull lodge poles and burdens with a travois.

DOG

DRINK

74. **DRINK:** Hold cupped right hand in front of face, then push upward to mouth to make motion of drinking. Also means *water*.

*DRUM: With thumb and index fingers of both hands form an incomplete circle, then with right hand holding an imaginary drum stick strike down toward half circle of left hand.*

*DUCK: Do bird sign, then hold fingers flat by nose to indicate broad bill, then do sign for water.*

*DULL: Hold left palm up, draw side of right hand, from left to right, slowly across left palm. Means* **dull knife cutting.**

75. **EAGLE:** Wave hands at side to indicate bird, then curve hand at nose to indicate eagle beak.

*EARRINGS: Hold index fingers downward at side of each ear.*

*EARTH: See land.*

EAGLE

EAT

**76. EAT:** Curve right hand, palm towards body, pull forward past lips and downward, several times. Means *pushing down food.*

**77. EFFORT:** Place closed hands in front of chest and strain to pull apart.

*EGG: Do sign for bird then make an oval shape with thumb and index finger and make sign for born.*

EFFORT

ELK

END

**78. ELK:** Touch thumbs to ears, fingers spread, raise hands upward and outward, then bend index finger and touch canine tooth on right side. *EMPTY: See hungry.*

**79. END:** Hold hands in vertical position, brush right palm across and downward on left palm. Means *cutting off.*

ENDURE

**80. ENDURE:** Slightly bend left hand and place on chest, hold right palm toward face and clench. Means *to suffer.*

EQUAL

EXTERMINATE

**81. EQUAL:** Close hands, extend index fingers slightly apart, move forward touching fingers together and sweep upward. Means *even, same* and *also.*

> *EVIL: See bad.*

**82. EXTERMINATE:** Hold left palm up, with right palm make brushing-like motions, from wrist towards fingers. Means *wiped out* or *destroyed.*

> *EYES: See I.*
> *FAIL: See cannot.*

**83. FAST:** Hold up left hand in vertical position, swiftly pass right fingers over left palm from right to left, touching the palm as you make the motion and swinging right hand upward.

FAST

FATHER

FIGHT

**84. FATHER:** With slightly curved right hand, tap right chest two or three times.

**85. FIGHT:** Clench hands. Push right away from body, pull back, then push left away from body, pull back. Repeat motions. Also means *war*.

FIRE

**86. FIRE:** Hold hands up in front of body, fingers slightly apart, open fingers upward and close downward several times. Means *flickering flame*.

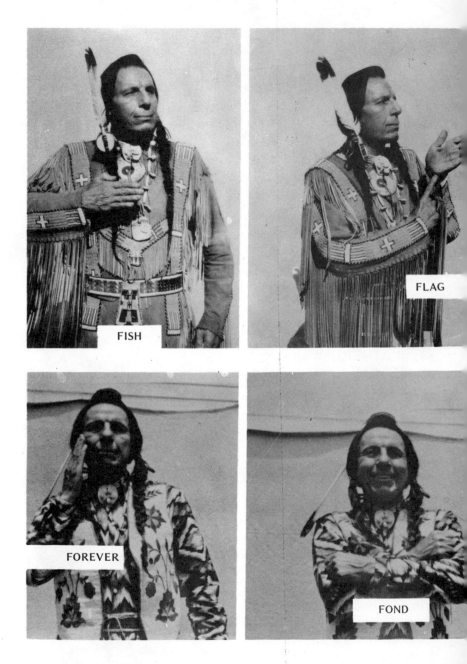

FISH

FLAG

FOREVER

FOND

87. **FISH:** Hold up right hand, palm facing body, make wavering-like motions. The sign for water can also be used.

88. **FLAG:** Hold left hand up in vertical position, place right index finger at base of wrist, wave left hand back and forth.

*FLOWER: Do the sign for grow by bringing right index finger upward in jerking-like motions, then place both palms together fingers outspread.*

*FOG: Do sign for water then cross hands, fingers outspread and place over eyes.*

89. **FOND:** Cross arms at wrists, clench hands, pull to body with left fist resting over heart.

*FOOD: See eat.*

*FOREST: Hold fingers apart, palms toward body, move slowly upward. Means* **trees growing.**

90. **FOREVER:** Place right palm to side of head, move hand backward and forward, twice.

*FORGET: With left hand, clasp right index finger. Pull right index finger downward.*

FOUND

FRIEND

FULL

GAP

91. **FOUND:** Pick up imaginary object with both hands, clench hands and raise above head. Means *"I have found it."*

92. **FRIEND:** At side hold up right index and middle fingers together, palm out, bring upward above shoulders. Means *two who have grown up together.* Some tribes shake their own hand to indicate friend.

FROG: *Do sign for water, then hold fingers together, thumb touching middle finger, then push forward in hopping-like motion.*

FRUIT: *Make sign for tree, then make a circle with thumb and index finger, and move here and there to indicate hanging fruit, then do sign for eat.*

93. **FULL:** Pull hand upward from stomach and place under chin, right thumb up.

94. **GAP:** Do sign for mountain, then pass side of right hand past thumb of vertical left hand. Also means *gorge or mountain pass.*

GET UP: *See arise*

GIRL: *See woman and little.*

GIVE

GO

GOAT

**95. GIVE:** Hold out right hand, palm towards face, lower hand and extend outward. Means *"I give you."*

*GIVE ME: Hold arm out palm up, pull in toward chest.*

**96. GO:** Hold vertical right hand forward and pointing slightly downward, swing forward and up.

*GO AWAY: Hold right hand up, palm forward, swing hand forward and then to the right in a slight curve. Repeat once or twice.*

**97. GOAT:** Hold grouped fingers extended downward under chin. Also means *beard*.

GOOD

**98. GOOD:** Place right hand, palm down, on left breast, then push away from body swinging upward. Means *heart is good.*

*GORGE: See gap.*

*GRANDFATHER: Do signs for old man and father.*

**99. GRASS:** Hold both hands down low, fingers upward and separated, swing hands slightly apart, then raise up slowly. Means *grass growing.*

*GREAT SPIRIT: See medicine.*

*GROUP: See patrol.*

GRASS

GUN

100. **GUN:** Position hands as if holding a gun, then do the sign for fire.

*HALF: Hold up left hand, palm toward body, place heel of right hand on middle knuckle of left index finger and move towards right past fingers.*

101. **HALF-BREED:** Touch middle of body with side of right hand, fingers up, then move hand slowly to left, then move to right, now use the sign for Indian or white man.

*HANG: Extend left index finger and hook right index finger over it, elbow down.*

*HAPPY: Do sign for heart, then with thumb and index fingers of right hand form an incomplete circle facing chest and slowly raise a few inches upward.* Means **sunshine in heart.**

HALF-BREED

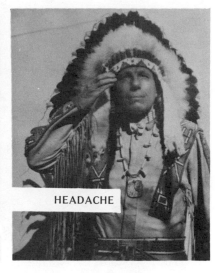

HARD

HEADACHE

**102. HARD:** Hit palm of left hand with right fist in a pounding-like motion. Also means *iron.*

*HAT: Hold right hand slightly above head in horizontal position with thumb out, bring down and rest thumb and index finger on forehead.*

HEAR

**103. HEADACHE:** With right index finger touch top of head then close hand and open and close fingers in front of forehead to indicate throbbing pain.

**104. HEAR:** Cup right hand and place to ear with palm forward. Also means *listen.*

HEART

HEAVEN

105. **HEART:** Place right hand on left chest, fingers downward, thumb touching body.

106. **HEAVEN:** Look up to sky and with right index finger point upwards.

*HEAVY: Hold hands out, palms up, raise slightly, then drop several inches.*

107. **HELLO:** Hold right hand erect, palm outward, make a circular motion toward the right, about eye level. Also means the greeting "How".

*HELP: Do signs for work and with.*

*HIDE: Extend left hand, palm down, fingers pointing at an angle from body, move right hand, palm down, under left hand.*

HELLO

HIGH

HILLS

**108. HIGH:** Hold right hand out, palm down fingers pointing outward, then raise hand up to indicate height.

**109. HILLS:** Hold clenched hands, shoulder high, palms toward body, move fists slightly up and down indicating uneven height of hills.

*HOLD: Hold left hand upward, close fingers, with right hand clasp wrist of left hand.*

*HONEST: See true.*

**110. HORSE:** Hold left hand in vertical position, place index and third fingers astride left hand. Make up and down motion to indicate sign of riding horse.

*HOT: See sun is hot.*

HORSE

HOUSE

HUNGRY

I

I'M SPEAKING

**111.  HOUSE:**  Hold hands up in front of chest, touch finger tips of both hands together, thumbs not touching.  To make sign for city, make sign for house, then do sign for many.

*HOW MANY?:  Do sign for question, then hold left hand up palm down, with right index finger press little finger down into hand and repeat with each finger, until all fingers are down.*

**112.  HUNGRY:**  Hold right palm up and make cutting motion across stomach two or three times.  Means *cut in half, everything gone, or empty.*

*HUNTING:  Look for sign see.*

*HURRY:  Do signs for work and fast.*

**113.  I:**  Point right thumb towards body, or with right index finger touch side of eye.  To say eyes, touch nose on each side with right index finger.

*IDEA:  Hold right index up to forehead, swing down to mouth and push forward and upward.  Means* "I **have a thought."**

*IMPOSSIBLE:  See cannot.*

**114.  I'M SPEAKING:**  Point to body with finger, then place closed hand near mouth and flick open the fingers two or three times.

INCREASE

INDIAN

**115. INCREASE:** Hold palms facing each other, fingers forward, jerk hands apart slowly to width of body. For a *great increase* hold palms one above the other and pull right hand upward.

**116. INDIAN:** With right hand rub back and forth on top of left hand. Indicate color of skin. If known, indicate tribe.

INFERIOR

**117. INFERIOR:** Hold right index lower than left finger, back of hands towards body. Means *not even* or *the same.*

INNOCENT

IN-LAW

**118. IN-LAW:** Place left hand on right shoulder, place right hand on left shoulder. Move right hand down from left wrist to elbow, add sign for woman and old, mother-in-law; man and old, father-in-law. Means *relative on side.*

**119. INNOCENT:** At side of shoulders hold hands up palms facing outward. Means *hands clean* or *nothing to hide.*

*INSIDE: Hold out left arm in shape of semi-circle. Group fingers of right hand and push downward through semi-circle.*

*IRON: See hard, then point to a metallic object.*

*IRON EYES: Do sign for iron then point with index finger to both eyes.*

**120. JEALOUS:** Clench fists in middle of body jerk away from each other. Means *el-bowing aside.*

JEALOUS

JOKE

JUMP

KEEP

**121. JOKE:** Cup right hand, fingers spread, in front of mouth, then push away from face.

*JOY: See happy.*

**122. JUMP:** Hold right palm down, group fingers together, push hand forward in jumping-like motion.

**123. KEEP:** Grasp left upright index finger with right hand, move slightly to right then back to left.

KEY

KILL

KNIFE

124. **KEY:** With thumb and forefinger of right hand, make motion of turning key in palm of left hand.

125. **KILL:** Close right hand hold back up to shoulder, push hand forward and downward to left side, opening and closing fingers two or three times.

126. **KNIFE:** Place palm over mouth and make a motion as though cutting meat off which is being held with teeth and left fingers.

KNOW

LAKE

**127. KNOW:** Close right hand over heart, extend thumb upward point index finger, other fingers closed, push out and away from body slightly upward.

**128. LAKE:** Do the sign for water and with thumb and index finger of both hands make a circle, then pull away from one another.

**129. LAND:** Extend hands in front of body, palms down, then push downward and pull away from one another. Also means *earth*.

LAND

*LARGE: See big.*
*LASSO: See rope.*

LAST ONE

LEAD

LIES

130. **LAST ONE:** Hold up left hand, thumb toward body, touch left thumb with right index finger.

*LATE: See after.*

*LAUGH: Hold slightly bent fingers, palms up, on either side of mouth, push hands up and down slightly.*

131. **LEAD:** Hold right clenched hand to right shoulder, as if holding a rope to lead a pony, pull forward with slight jerks.

132. **LIES:** Extend right index and middle fingers, pass in vertical position across mouth in sweeping motion. Means *forked tongue of a snake.*

LIGHTNING

LITTLE

133. **LIGHTNING:** Hold right index finger up by side of head, make a quick zigzag downward to imitate lightning. *LISTEN: See hear.*

LIVER

134. **LITTLE:** Close right hand, with thumb touch first knuckle of index finger. Also means *small.*

135. **LIVER:** Place right hand on side below ribs, then shake hand back and forth vigorously near side.

LOGS

LONG

LOVE

**136. LOGS:** Spread fingers of both hands in vertical position, insert fingers between each other. To make log house, form an angle with fingers.

**137. LONG:** Hold index fingers paralled, push left index finger forward, pull right index finger backwards towards right.

*LOOK: Do sign for see.*

**138. LOVE:** Man crosses arms over chest. Woman touches her heart. Also means *fond.*

*MAD: See angry.*

*MAKE: See work.*

MAN

MANY TIMES

MARRY

**139. MAN:** Hold up right index finger, palm out, at level of chin.   Also means *male*.

*MANY: Hold up hands, elbows at sides, fingers pointing outward, bend fingers slightly, drop hands down and bring in to one another, ending with a small space between.*

**140. MANY TIMES:** Extend left hand palm downwards. With right index finger touch wrist and move finger an inch at a time up towards elbow.

**141. MARRY:** Quickly bring index fingers together, side by side,   Also means *we are together.*

*MATCH: With imaginary match held in right hand scratch down left forearm.*

*ME: With thumb of right hand point to body.*

*MEAN: See bad.*

MEAT

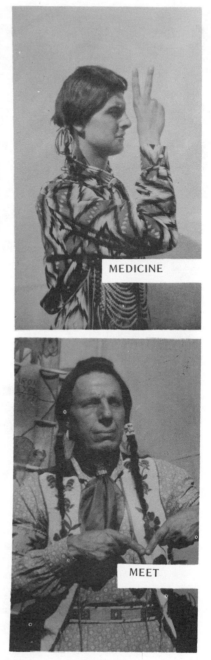

MEDICINE

MEET

142. **MEAT:** Do sign for buffalo or deer. Hold left hand in vertical position and then hold left hand with thumb across palm and fingers in back to indicate thickness.

143. **MEDICINE:** Separate right index and middle fingers and hold close to forehead, then spiral upward. Means *great spirit, mysterious* and *unknown.*

144. **MEET:** Touch tips of index fingers together.
    *MEMORY: Do signs for heart* and *know.*

MEMORIES

MINGLE

MOOSE

**145. MEMORIES:** Lower head and place fist under chin.
*MIDDLE: See center.*

**146. MINGLE:** Hold fingers up, slightly apart and bent, palms facing each other. Rotate hands in imaginary circle.
*MIRROR: Hold right palm, fingers upward, toward face. Represents hand mirror.*
*MONEY: See coin.*
*MOON: Do sign for night, then hold up right thumb and index finger in the shape of a crescent. Means* **night sun.**

**147. MOOSE:** Hold hands, palms out fingers together, at each side of head, then move hands out, up and away from head.

MOTHER

MUD

148. **MOTHER:** Tap left breast two or three times with fingers of right hand.

*MOUNTAIN PASS: See gap.*

149. **MUD:** Hold grouped fingers of right hand with left hand, pull right hand out of left. Reverse hands and repeat motion. Means *animal pulling feet out of mud.* Also *point to ground.*

150. **MULE:** Hold hands by ears, fingers up, palms facing out. With wrist action move hands forward and back.

*MULTIPLY: See add.*

*MUST: See push.*

*MYSTERIOUS: See medicine.*

*NAMED: See called.*

MULE

NARROW

NEAR

NEXT

**151. NARROW:** Hold palms facing in vertical position and a few inches apart, bring hands together, leaving only a very narrow space between them.

**152. NEAR:** Hold up right hand, palm toward shoulder, pull in slightly down toward body.

**153. NEXT:** Hold out left hand, palm down. With right index finger move left index finger to the right, then with right index finger touch the middle finger of left hand.

NEZ PERCE

NIGHT

154. **NEZ PERCE:** Do sign for Indian then with right index finger push under nose. Means *pierced nose*.

155. **NIGHT:** Hold out hands, palms down, pass right hand over left hand making a shadow.

NO

156. **NO:** Hold right hand towards body fingers pointing to left; push hand away from body in a wide half circle turning the palm up and fingers pointing outward.

NOW

OLD MAN

OSAGE

OTTER

157. **NOW:** Hold right index finger in front of face, quickly push finger forward a few inches and stop, then pull finger back slightly.

*NUMBERS: See counting on page 104.*

*OATH: With fingers of right hand tap heart, then hold up hand, shoulder high, palm facing outward.*

*OBEY: Do sign for listen then add sign for yes.*

*OFTEN: See many times.*

158. **OLD MAN:** Close right hand and lean on imaginary cane and bend body slightly. Do sign of man.

*ON: Lay right palm on back of left palm, fingers a-head.*

*ONION: Hold clenched fist down low, back up, pinch nose for smell then do sign for bad.*

*OPEN: Place palms together, fingers pointing outward, open hands keeping little fingers touching.*

159. **OSAGE:** Place backs of hands on back of head, fingers pointing toward each other, pull hands up and down as if shaving off hair. They were called *"Shave heads."*

160. **OTTER:** Place two fingers by ear and spiral downward. The Plains Indians decorated their hair with strips of otter skin.

OUT OF

OVERTAKE

**161. OUT OF:** Bend left arm, palm down, pass slightly bent hand over left arm.
*OVER: See across.*

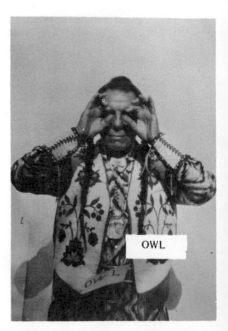

OWL

**162. OVERTAKE:** Hold out left hand, palm out and fingers pointing upward. Touch back of left hand with right index finger.

**163. OWL:** Do sign for bird, then touch thumb and index fingers together to make circles and place over eyes. Means *big eyes.*

PARDON

PARALLEL

**164. PAINT:** With fingers of right hand rub the palm of the left hand, or with right fingers rub right cheek.

**165. PARALLEL:** Point index fingers forward, palms down, leaving a space between. Means *side by side.*

**166. PARDON:** Hold thumbs and index fingers up by shoulders, palms out, push up past head and circle down and ending with index fingers pointing out and slightly downward. Do sign for go. Means *removing a halter.*

*PASSING THROUGH:* See *canyon.*

PAINT

PATROL

PEACE

**167. PATROL:** Hold up left hand, fingers bunched together, grasp fingers with right thumb and index finger, letting fingers of left hand stick out. Also means *group* or *band of people.*

*PAWNEE INDIAN: See wolf.*

PEAK

**168. PEACE:** Clasp hands in front of body. Means *my hands are empty.*

**169. PEAK:** Hold up right hand, bunch fingers together, palm toward body.

PIPE

PEOPLE

170. **PEOPLE:** Hold up fingers, palms out, move up and down to indicate different sizes. Or hold up all fingers, palms out, and move up and down.

171. **PIPE:** Point right index finger to mouth with thumb up, other fingers closed.

172. **PISTOL:** Do sign for gun, then hold up thumb of right hand and five fingers of left hand. Means *"Six Shooter."*

PISTOL

PITY

POOR

POSSESSIONS

**173. PITY:** Place index fingers, palm out, by heart, push forward and downward towards person. For pity me, extend index fingers, palms up, and pull toward heart.

*PLANT: See sit down.*

**174. POOR:** Scrape left index finger with right index finger. Means *scraping to the bone.*

**175. POSSESSION:** Hold clenched hand by shoulder, swing hand down in horizontal position, thumb pointing forward. Means *it is mine, it belongs to me.*

*POTATO: Hold fist down low with back up.*

PREACHER

PRIDE

**176. PREACHER:** Place palms of hands on chest, sweep hands down as low as possible. Means *robe*. Point to something black.

*PRETTY: Hold up right hand as if looking into a mirror, then do sign for good.*

**177. PRIDE:** Place right palm over mouth, throw head back, then do the sign for good.

**178. PRISONER:** Close both hands and place right wrist over left wrist and push down. Means *hands bound*.

PRISONER

PRIVATE TALK

PUSH

**179. PRIVATE TALK:** Hold left hand in front of mouth, place right hand near left and open and close fingers several times  Also means *secret*.

QUARREL

**180. PUSH:** Place fists at sides near breast, push hands forward with an effort.

**181. QUARREL:** Wave index fingers back and forth in front of face.  Means *two people arguing*.

QUESTION

QUIET DOWN

182. **QUESTION:** Hold up right hand, palm facing outward and fingers slightly bent, shake hand back and forth by wrist movement.

*QUICK: See fast.*

183. **QUIET DOWN:** Hold up right hand palm forward, push hand down gently two or three times.

*RACE: Hold index fingers parallel to one another, push both forward very fast.*

184. **RAIN:** Hold up hands by head, fingers hanging down loosely, push down spreading fingers to indicate falling rain.

RAIN

RASH

READ

REMEMBER

185. **RASH:** Place left palm over eyes, point right index forward. Means *going ahead blindly*, or *foolish*.

186. **READ:** Hold palm of left hand upward, with right index finger pointing at wrist line; move finger towards tips of left hand, repeat two or three times.

187. **REMEMBER:** Hold up right index finger, clasp finger with left hand. Remember not to pull right index down from left hand.

*RISE: Extend right index finger, palm up, raise to shoulder height. Means to* **come up.**

RISING MAN

RISING SUN

**188. RISING MAN:** Clench left hand, palm out in front of chest, place right index finger at base of left thumb, push right finger up until wrist is beside top of hand. Means *man becoming famous.*

**189. RISING SUN:** Form half circle with thumb and index finger hold at center of body then raise slowly upward.

**190. RIVER:** Do sign for water and with right index finger, palm towards body, pull across from left to right, making an up and down movement with finger.

*ROCK: Do sign for hard then indicate shape with thumb and index finger.*

RIVER

Iron Eyes shows
Ken Mansker sign
for ROPE

ROLL

191.  ROLL:  Hold hands erect, palms facing one another, curve fingers slightly and roll imaginary object between them two or three times.

RUN AGAINST

192.  ROPE:  Do sign for after, then make a spiralling-like motion towards your right side. Iron Eyes doing sign for Artist Ken Mansker.

193.  RUN AGAINST:  Hold up left hand, fingers pointing out, strike palm of left hand with back of right hand. Means *in a fix* or *run up against*.

RUN AWAY

194. **RUN AWAY:** Hold up left hand, palm down and thumb towards body, quickly push right index finger under left hand from right to left. Means *to sneak away* or *hide out.*

*SAD:* Do sign for heart then bring hand forward, turning so the palm is up, and move hand down low. Means **my heart is on the ground.**

195. **SADDLE:** Hold hands erect, palms facing each other, place wrists of hands together, fingers clenched and held away from each other.

SADDLE

SALT

196. **SALT:** Touch tongue with right forefinger then do sign for bad. This sign is also used for bitter and sour. A sprinkling motion may be added for salt.

*SAME: See equal.*
*SCARED:    See afraid.*
*SCOUT: See wolf.*
*SECRET:    See private talk.*

197. **SEE:** Separate index and middle finger of right hand, place by right eye, then push forward. For hunting, do above sign and zigzag fingers forward.

**SEIZE:** *With both hands reach out and grab an imaginary object and pull back towards body.*

*SELECT:    See choose.*

SEE

SEPARATE

SETTING SUN

**198.  SEPARATE:**  Close hands, palms down, extend index fingers side by side, pull right index towards right, left index towards left, forming a v-shape.

**199.  SETTING SUN:**  Form half circle with thumb and index fingers of right hand, move downward,  starting at face level.

SEW

**200.  SEW:**  Use right index finger like a needle and push between thumb and index finger of left hand.  Also means *awl*.

**201.  SHARP:**  Extend left hand, palm up.  Starting at the side of the wrist of left hand, run thumb and index finger of right hand up to the little finger, then make the sign for good.

*SHEEP:  Slightly curved hands with fingers pointing to head above each eye, then make a sweeping motion back and downward then out past face to indicate the curve of the horns.*

**202.  SHOOT BOW:**  Grasp imaginary bow with left hand, with right fingers pull imaginary string backwards toward the right.

*SHORT:  Hold right palm towards body, fingers pointing up, draw downward about five inches.  Means* **something short.**

**203.  SHOSHONE:**  Make a snake-like motion across body with right index finger, from left to right.  Do sign for Indian.  First motion also means *snake*.  Some tribes make a snake-like motion forward to indicate snake.

*SHRINK:  See afraid.*

*SICK:  See ache.*

**204.  SILENT:**  Place right index finger to lips.  To say "shut up!" place all upright fingers over mouth.

*SING:  Hold right index and middle fingers apart, other fingers closed, place near mouth with fingers slanted upward.  Swing fingers up and out to right and around and back to mouth in a small circle.*

*SINK:  See die.*

SIOUX

SIT DOWN

SLEEP

SNO

**205. SIOUX:** Do sign for Indian then with right hand, palm down, make a cutting motion across throat. Means *cut throats.*

**206. SIT DOWN:** Place fist of right hand over fist of left hand, then push both fists downward. Also means *plant.*

    *SKY: Point to heavens with right index finger.*

    *SLED: Turn palms up, extend index fingers, closing others, make half circle of index fingers and push forward.*

**207. SLEEP:** Place palms together, bend head to left, then lay back of right hand on left cheek.

    *SLOW: Palms facing each other, fingers ahead with small space between hands, slowly move left hand forward, then slowly move right hand forward. Repeat.*

    *SMOKE: For smoke of signal fire, do sign for fire, then slowly spiral hand upward.*

    *SNAKE: See Shoshone.*

    *SNEAK: See run away.*

**208. SNOW:** Spread fingers of both hands as in rain, then gently, and slowly zigzag hands downward.

    *SORROW: See sad.*

**209. SPEAK:** Hold closed hand near mouth, flick open the fingers two or three times. Means *throwing voice out.* Also means *talk.*

*SPIDER: Near a flat surface spread fingers, palm down, then move fingers like a spider walking.*

*SPRING: Do sign for water, then sign for lake, then holding left hand in semi-circle bring bunched right fingers up through opening and flick fingers open.* Means **bubbling spring.**

**210. STEAL:** With right index finger make a hook-like motion towards the right under the left palm. Means *taking.*

**211. STRONG:** Clench both hands tight, then make a twisting motion, one over the other, as if trying to break a stick.

*SUFFER: See endure.*

*SUGAR: Touch tongue with right index finger then make the sign for good.*

**212. SUN IS HOT:** Hold hands over head, pull down towards head two or three times.

SUPERIOR

SURRENDER

**213. SUPERIOR:** Hold right index finger slightly higher than left index finger, palms facing outward. Higher finger means *better man.*

*SURPRISED: See astonished.*

**214. SURRENDER:** Hold hands upward by shoulders, palms facing outward.

*SWIFT: See fast.*

*TAKE: Extend right index finger, palm down, turn palm in and hook finger toward body.*

*TALK: See speak.*

TASTE

**215. TASTE:** Touch tongue with right index finger.

TELEPHONE

TENT

**216. TELEPHONE:** Hold hand to ear and do sign for wire by pulling index finger across body, then do sign for talk. Means *talking wire.*

**217. TENT:** Touch tips of index fingers together, then add sign for white man.

    *THANK YOU: Extend right hand, palm toward person, bring down so palm is facing down and fingers are pointing outward. Two hands are used to give extra thanks.*

    *THERE: Point middle finger.*

**218. THINK:** Point right index finger and place over heart, thumb touching body, pull away a few inches, keeping palm down. Means *from the heart.*

THINK

THROUGH

TOBACCO

TOMAHAWK

**219.  THROUGH:** Hold up left hand, pass side of right hand between middle and third fingers.

*TIPI: Cross index fingers at first joint.*

*TIRED: See weary.*

**220.  TOBACCO:** Rub left palm with clenched right hand in a circular motion. Means *breaking up leaves.*

*TODAY: Do sign for day and sign for now.*

*TOGETHER: See marry.*

**221.  TOMAHAWK:** Hold right elbow with left hand, make chopping motions with right hand from left shoulder down to left elbow.

TRADE

TREE

222. **TRADE:** Cross index fingers in front of one another. Some tribes pass open hands in front of one another.

223. **TREE:** Hold up right hand, palm towards body, spread fingers, move upward slowly, to indicate growth. Hold up both hands for trees; to indicate a forest, use both hands and add sign of many.

*TROOP: See patrol.*

224. **TRUE:** Place right index finger by chin, finger pointing out, push forward in a straight line. Means *straight talk.*

*TRY: See effort.*
*TWINS: See alike.*

TRUE

UGLY

UP

US

225. **UGLY:** Pass palm of hand over face then do sign for bad.

    *UNABLE: See cannot.*
    *UNDER: See below.*
    *UNDERSTAND: See know.*

226. **UP:** Hold up right index finger, palm out and chest high, bring up to face level.

227. **US:** Close hand and point thumb to body, then do sign for all.

WAGON

228. **WAGON:** Form half circle with thumb and index fingers, backs down, roll forward and outward. Means *wheels*. For covered wagon, do above sign then cup hands together fingers touching, palms down, pull apart and circle downward, ending with palms facing at sides.

*WAIT: Hold up right hand, shoulder high and palm facing out, bring down to horizontal position. Repeat. To signal halt, do above sign, but bring hand to a quick stop.*

229. **WALK:** With hands parallel to each other and palms down, move one hand forward, drop slightly and pull back, then repeat with other hand in walking motion. Do two or three times.

WALK

WANT

230. **WANT:** Form incomplete circle with right thumb and index finger, other fingers closed, back of hand towards right, bring towards mouth and pull downward.

*WAR: See sign for fight.*

231. **WATCH:** (clock) Form a circle with left thumb and index fingers. Tap around imaginary numbers in clockwise motion.

*WATER: See drink.*

WATCH

WEARY

WELL

232. **WEARY:** Place index fingers side by side, curve slightly and push slowly downward. Also means *tired*.

233. **WELL:** Place open hands on chest, pointing towards each other, pull to sides while closing hands, then push down with a slight jerk. Means *body strong*.

234. **WHEN:** Do sign for question, then hold up index fingers, others closed, with right index point to tip of left index and trace a small circle around it; stop and touch tip of finger.

WHEN

WHITE MAN

WITH

235. **WHITE MAN:** Move right index finger across forehead from left to right. This indicates brim of a hat.

*WIDE: See big.*

236. **WITH:** Hold left palm vertically; bring right index finger into horizontal position and place in center of hand with finger pointing outward.

237. **WOLF:** Hold up in v-shape right index and middle fingers, palm forward, near shoulder, bring up to ear and wave slightly. To say scout do above sign but do not wave fingers. This sign is used to say *Pawnee Indian.*

WOLF

238. **WOMAN:** Make comb-ing-like motions with fingers downward through hair. Place closed hands by chin and pull down to indicate long hair or braids. Touch cheek with right hand to indicate rough on face.

239. **WORK:** Hold hands in vertical position, palms facing each other, pull right hand back to about the center of left hand, move by wrist mo-tion up and down, two or three times.

*WORLD: Do signs for all and land.*

WRITE

**240. WRITE:** Hold imaginary pencil in right hand and make motion as if writing across left palm.

*WRONG: See bad.*

*YEAR: Do sign for snow then with right index finger pointing outward swing it upward then down towards the left side then back up to the right side, making an imaginary circle in front of chest, then repeat snow sign. This means* **one snow.** *Most tribes called a year one winter or one snow.*

**241. YELL:** Place closed hand by mouth open fingers and push forward vigorously. Meaning sound coming out of mouth.

YELL

YES

YESTERDAY

242. **YES:** Hold up right index finger, bend, pull rapidly downward towards body. Or you can simply nod your head.

243. **YESTERDAY:** Do sign for night, then hold left hand palm down, next pull right hand away, twisting wrist so right palm is up, then pass under and beyond left hand.

244. **YOU:** Point right index finger towards person. For choose or select, push finger forward to person or object.

YOU

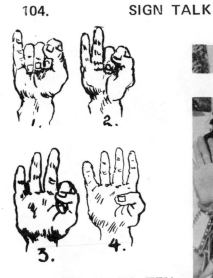

COUNT OF TEN

**245. COUNTING TO TEN:**
Hold up both hands palms out,
close hands, starting with the
right hand extend the little finger upward, the next finger for
two, and so on with the rest
of the fingers including the
thumbs.

**246. COUNT OF TEN:** Hold
up both hands, palms out, fingers apart, push hands downward.

*COUNTING TO ONE
HUNDRED: Use count of ten
sign and make a sweeping motion from left to right, thumbs
touching.*

*COUNTING TO FIFTY:
Hold out left hand palm down,
fingers outspread. With right
index touch each finger including thumb. Each finger represents the count of ten.*

COUNTING TO 100

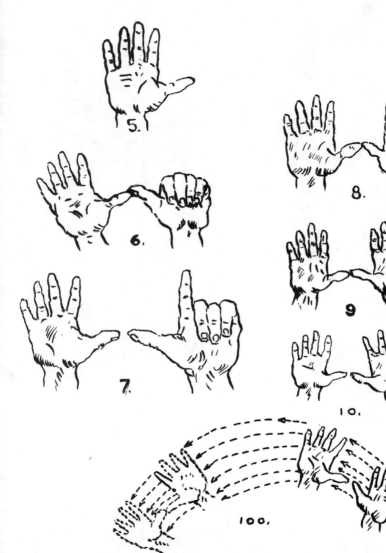

5.

6.

7.

8.

9.

10.

100,

MANSKER

7 SCOUTS

SEVEN

SCOUTS

(NIGHT COVERS OVER)

EAT

BACON TONIGHT

HUNTERS

(ACT OF SHOOTING BOW & ARROW)

BIG

SEPARATE HANDS WIDE

FATHER

and MY

TAP RIGHT BREAST SEVERAL TIMES

CHIEF OVER HIS

KILLS

CAST DOWN VIGOROUSLY

FIRE IN CAMP

RAIN

## PICTURE WRITING

The American Indian had no written language and one early form of recording a message or an event was by means of pictographs. The Plains Indian tribes recorded certain events by painting symbols on animal hides. I designed and made up the two examples shown here and my good Scouter friend Ed Olin did the drawings.

ED.OLIN

Reading from center outward: Two Brothers, Cheyenne Indian Buffalo hunters, walked four days, roped two fast horses, then traveled over mountains and through a forest, crossed a river and camped for the night near some hills. They heard buffalo that day, killed some, then traveled back to their camp and hung the meat to dry on the racks.

## PICTURE WRITING

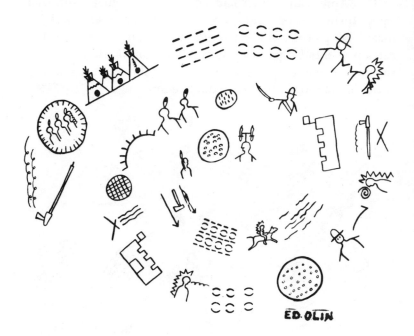

ED OLIN

Reading from center outward: Chief Two Knife and many Indians are going to war on horses. They travel to a fort where a few soldiers are stationed. The Indians waited all day for night and camped near the fort. The chief heard horses and many soldiers coming to the fort that day. The chief thought it over and at the fort they talked peace and smoked the pipe. All the Indians and horses went back to their camp and held a peace council.

Interior views of author's "Moosehead Museum."

For further information it is suggested that the following books be consulted:

Clarke, Capt. W.P., *Indian Sign Language,* pub. by Hamersly & Co., Phila., 1885.

Cody, Iron Eyes, *How Indian Sign Talk in Pictures,* pub. by Homer H. Boelter Lithography, Los Angeles, Calif. Out of Print.

Mallery, Col. Garrick, *Gesture Signs and Signals of the North American Indian,* pub. by Bureau of American Ethnology, Smithsonian Institution, 1881.

Seton, Ernest Thompson, *Sign Talk* . . . pub. by Doubleday, Page & Co., New York, 1918. A good bibliography on the subject.

Tomkins, William, *Universal Indian Sign Language,* pub. by the author, San Diego, Calif., 1926.

MOTHER

CAT

WANT

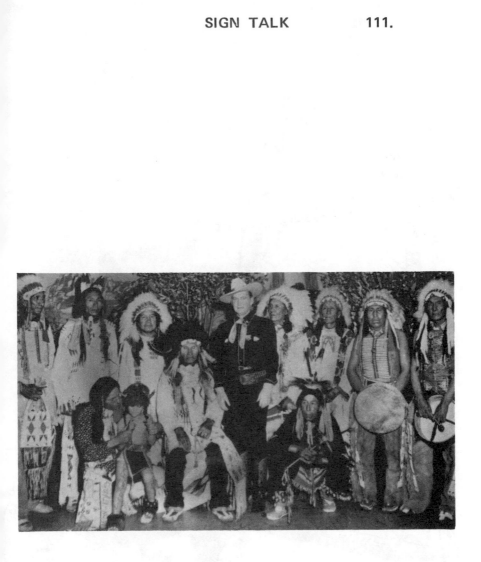

Group of Sioux Indians from South Dakota. Iron Eyes holding boy called Little Iron, John Sitting Bull, with horned headdress, Colonel Tim McCoy, famous movie star, and to his left Frank Andrew Foolscrow, medicine-man.

John was 92 years old when this picture was taken, his father was the famous Chief Sitting Bull. His only means of communication was by sign language.

Frank Foolscrow is my adopted brother through a ceremonial Uwipi ritual.